# 7 Mistakes to Avoid for Online Business Success

*Proven Strategies to Enhance Your Online Business Performance.*

Ross M. Chaney

Copyright© 2024 Ross M. Chaney All rights reserved.

This work is protected by copyright law and may not be reproduced, distributed, transmitted, displayed, published, or broadcast without the prior written permission of the copyright holder.

Unauthorized use, duplication, or dissemination of this work is strictly prohibited and may result in legal action.

# Table Of Content

INTRODUCTION

1 NOT TREATING YOUR ONLINE BUSINESS AS A PROPER BUSINESS

2 NOT HAVING A PLAN

3 NOT CHOOSING THE RIGHT NICHE

4 NOT THE THE RIGHT ONLINE BUSINESS MODEL

5 THE SHINY OBJECT SYNDROME

6 NOT GETTING ENOUGH TRAFFIC

7 NOT TESTING AND ANALYZING RESULTS
CONCLUSION

# INTRODUCTION

It is extremely simple to start an internet company. However, if you don't approach things appropriately, you'll never succeed. Many individuals who start an internet company give it up after a short period. It would be beneficial if you did not do the same.

In this powerful article, we will highlight the seven pitfalls you must avoid in your internet company. When you avoid these blunders, you will have a far better chance of succeeding with your internet company.

# 1 NOT TREATING YOUR ONLINE BUSINESS AS A PROPER BUSINESS

Most individuals start an internet company out of curiosity. They've read a lot of outrageous promises about how they can earn a fortune with a few mouse clicks, so they acquire a domain name and some hosting and start playing about.

They adhere to the guidelines provided in any training program that promises them the world. Claims of quick traffic, and all that nonsense. When they realize there is no such thing as generating a fortune in their undies by clicking their mouse and employing "miracle software," they quickly lose interest and give up.

The fact is that starting an internet company is rather inexpensive. A domain name costs around $10 per year, and site hosting is $10 per month. If you install the WordPress blogging software, you can create a website for free. With so little involved, it's no surprise that so many individuals abandon up when they learn it's not as simple as they thought.

If you don't approach your internet company like a legitimate business, you're far more likely to fail. You do not have to commit a lot of money, but you must make an emotional investment in your internet company.

Setting up an internet company is relatively simple; making it a success is tough. Regardless of what others say, building a strong and sustained internet company requires effort. To ensure effective functionality, you will need to invest in solutions such as an autoresponder service.

You must think that you are generating an asset. The website you create is your asset. As an exit plan, you may sell your website to a willing buyer for a significant fee. If you wish to sell your internet company after it is profitable, there will be several individuals interested.

To have a successful internet company, you must work on it every day. Forget the bullshit about miraculous software. You must learn to do the proper things and constantly promote your web company.

If you treat your internet company as a hobby or a trend, your prospects of success are slim. Consider investing your life savings in a physical store in your neighborhood mall. Would you consider it a pastime or a fad? No, you wouldn't, so assume you've put your life savings into your web company.

There may be days when everything goes wrong with your internet company. Something will cease functioning, or the campaigns you are doing will not provide the results you expect. To overcome these challenges and go on, you must be resilient and committed. Treating your internet company as if it were a genuine business can help you achieve this.

# 2 NOT HAVING A PLAN

How many individuals who start an internet company do you believe have a business plan? The answer is extremely few. Nobody knows how many internet firms fail each year, but the number will be high. Most new internet company owners do not establish objectives or develop a strategy. They are startled when everything fails.

If you want to establish an internet company, define a goal. The simplest objective to establish is a financial one. Consider how much revenue you want your internet company to make in the first 12 months and set it as your financial objective.

You're probably establishing an internet company because you feel it will provide you the independence you want. This is good, because a successful internet company may provide you with independence. No more working a dead-end job and spending hours commuting.

Your internet company has the potential to generate a lot of income. The only thing standing in the way is you. So, utilize the SMART goal-setting method to establish your objectives. If you're unfamiliar with this method, here's what it means:

***clear*** - your aim must be clear. For example, my internet company will create $100,000 during the next year.

***Measurable:*** You must be able to track your progress toward your objective. Fortunately, there are several techniques available to determine the performance of your internet company.

***Achievable;*** disregard the hype. It is quite improbable that you will earn a million dollars in your first year. Not impossible, however.

***Realistic*** - consider the time you have available and other resources, such as money.

**Timed -** You must set a time limit to your objective, such as a year. Open-ended objectives are meaningless.

After you've chosen your objective, you'll need to devise a strategy to reach it. You want to end up with a daily list of things that you can work on to get closer to your objective. So consider the macro activities in your strategy and then break them down into daily microtasks.

A basic plan would be:

Decide on the niche and online business strategy.

Set up the webpage.

Add content and find deals to promote.

Promote

Of course, they are high-level activities that will need subtasks to complete. You may get started right away by deciding on the specialty into which you wish to go. Write down your objectives and ambitions and keep them with you wherever you go.

# 3 NOT CHOOSING THE RIGHT NICHE

You should carefully examine the niche for your internet company. If you do this incorrectly, you might waste a lot of time, effort, and money while getting very little in return. There are hundreds of niches, but not all are suitable for an internet company.

Many tips on starting an internet company will urge you to pursue your interests. There is a noble aim behind this. If you establish an internet company in a niche that you are passionate about, you will be more determined to see it succeed.

That is OK if the topic you are passionate about has the potential to earn you a lot of money. You may be enthusiastic about sheep shearing in the Outback, but how many others will be?

When deciding on a specialty, you should consider two factors:

Is there demand?

Is there money in this niche?

If the answer is "no" to any of these questions, you should look for another specialization. The free Google Keyword Planner may help you determine the demand for a certain area. Simply add some seed keywords related to your expertise, such as "drone photography", and see how many searches this and comparable phrases get each month. The greater the number of searches, the better.

To discover whether there is money in the niche, enter a seed keyword and do a Google search. Are there many advertisements on the first page of the search results? If there are, it is a positive indication that money may be produced.

You may also utilize the website OfferVault.com to search for available deals based on your seed term. If there are a lot, you're probably on to a winner. There are certain areas where you can be certain that there will be a high level of demand and several prospects for profit. In our perspective, the top three are:

Health and fitness: weight reduction, etc.

Wealth creation: making money online, investing, etc.

Personal growth includes improved relationships, meeting boys and girls, self-improvement, and so on.

If you're not sure which specialty to pursue, follow the money. Don't worry if you're not an expert in the field right now. You can learn to master it. This is preferable to selecting an incorrect niche in which you are an expert and enthusiastic.

# 4 NOT THE THE RIGHT ONLINE BUSINESS MODEL

There are various Internet business models to select from. Here are several examples:

Affiliate marketing.

- CPA Marketing
- Sell your goods and services.
- Freelance services.
- Dropshipping
- Dropservicing
- Amazon FBA

- Your E-Commerce Store

- Self-publishing

You must choose the appropriate Internet business strategy for your situation. To start an e-commerce business or participate in Amazon FBA, you will need to invest some money in goods to sell. Do you have this money available? If not, you could borrow it, but you'd be taking a risk.

If you don't have much free time, it will be difficult to create and market your items and services. You can outsource product development, but this will cost you a significant amount of money.

Do you have a certain ability that is in demand? Here are some freelancing skills that are always in demand:

- SEO-optimized content authoring

- Copywriting

- Graphic Design (Logos, etc.)
- Programming
- Web Design and Development
- Creating mobile apps
- Search engine optimization
- Social media marketing.

If you have any of these abilities, you may sell them and earn a nice living online. You must be disciplined if you want to achieve this since your consumers will demand high-quality work delivered on schedule.
Affiliate marketing is perhaps the simplest internet business to start. If you're not sure what this is, the premise is straightforward. Many goods suppliers will give you a commission if you promote and endorse their items.

All you have to do is join up for their affiliate network and direct targeted visitors to the offer. When someone purchases via your affiliate link, you will get a commission from the product provider.

You may market both physical and digital items. Physical things are simpler to market, but commissions are often minimal. It is more difficult to offer digital things, but commissions are often significantly bigger.

There are affiliate networks that may help you locate deals to promote. If you are interested in tangible things, consider joining the Amazon Associates Program. You may discover hundreds of things to market, but you'll only earn 3% to 5% commission.

If you prefer digital items, you may join Clickbank.com or Digistore24.com to locate products with commissions of 50% or more. One thing to keep in mind is that since affiliate marketing is so simple, there are many internet company owners doing it, therefore you will have competition.

Do you have the newest popular book on your mind? If yes, you may write your book and self-publish it on sites like Amazon Kindle and Barnes & Noble. Nonfiction books may also be written and sold using self-publishing platforms.

Dropshipping is when you sell actual things on your website and have a dropshipping provider fulfill all of your orders for your consumers. You do not need to acquire any stock since you are just promoting the items offered by the dropshipping firm. Commissions are low in this industry, therefore you must sell a large number of things to earn a profit.

Dropservicing is a relatively new name, yet the notion has existed for many years. It is called service arbitrage, and it involves buying a service from a freelancer at a cheap cost and selling it to the consumer at a higher price.

All of these Internet business strategies have the potential to generate a lot of revenue. You must select the one that is best for you and stick to it. There is a lot to learn about each of these models. Don't switch between multiple Internet business models; this will never provide you with the results you seek.

# 5 THE SHINY OBJECT SYNDROME

The grass always seems greener over there. You've undoubtedly heard the word before. It suggests that your internet company has higher chances of success elsewhere. We refer to this as the "shiny object syndrome".

When you pick an online business model, some individuals will tell you that you made the incorrect decision and that you should switch to another program and pay for their training to teach you how to earn a fortune with it.

Many individuals who choose the wealth-building niche (making money online) are continuously assaulted with fresh dazzling goods that distract them. Every day, new courses and programs are introduced in this sector. All of them will advise you to quit what you're doing and follow their example.

We highly encourage you to avoid the shiny object syndrome, regardless of how appealing another offer seems. Some individuals buy these new "wonder methods" regularly because they feel the best remedy is just around the horizon.

They have hundreds of courses sitting on their hard drive, collecting digital dust. Some folks purchase these things but never open them! You don't want to get caught up in this downward spiral. Simply concentrate on what you're doing and do it to the best of your abilities.

We're not suggesting you shouldn't invest in further training for your chosen company strategy. You should understand as much as you can about it and be willing to attempt various approaches to make it work. However, you should resist shifting the route totally since the grass seems greener over there.

# 6 NOT GETTING ENOUGH TRAFFIC

What do you think is the key reason why the majority of internet companies fail? Could it be a lack of interest? Lack of resources? Don't have the greatest Internet connection? In our judgment, none of these items would apply. The solution is:

There's not enough traffic!

If you do not attract targeted visitors to your offerings, you will not generate any money online. You may promote a lousy deal and yet earn big money if you attract enough people to it.

On the other side, you might have the finest deal in the world, but if you don't provide enough targeted visitor traffic, you won't sell much, if at all. Traffic is the most vital part of any internet company, regardless of the model you pick.

If you are a freelancer and no one knows about your services, your web company will collapse. As an affiliate marketer, if you do not bring enough traffic to the items you promote, you will not get any commissions. You will not be able to sell anything if your e-commerce business does not get enough visitors.

Once you've established your internet company, you should devote the bulk of your time to marketing it. There are various options for doing this. If you don't want to invest money, consider content marketing, video marketing, social media marketing, and so on.

If you have a little budget, sponsored advertising might help you market your web company. You may buy pay-per-click (PPC) traffic from search engines like Google and Bing.

Alternatively, you may use social media advertisements to promote your company.

We recommend that you choose a combination of free and paid marketing. Email marketing is an effective approach to stay in contact with prospective consumers and encourage them to make a purchase. You will need to invest in an autoresponder service and create your email list, but if done correctly, it will pay off handsomely.

Nothing matters more than traffic creation. No traffic equals no business. So, commit to constantly promoting your web company. The more visitors you have, the more money you are likely to earn.

# 7 NOT TESTING AND ANALYZING RESULTS

One of the primary benefits of an Internet company over a traditional brick-and-mortar corporation is the ability to measure almost everything in real time. Many internet company owners, however, neglect or underutilize this.

If you want to see how many visits your website received last week, you may use a tool like Google Analytics. You can also determine where your visitors came from and which pages of your website they saw.

It's also essential to know how long they stayed on your site. This is referred to as the "bounce rate," and you want your visitors to remain as long as possible. If people are departing rapidly, you should investigate and address the issue.

You can and should monitor everything. This is particularly true if you are spending money on purchased traffic. You may use tracking codes to determine how many times a link has been clicked, among other things.

Nowadays, most social media sites provide sophisticated analytics services. You may use these to determine which of your posts perform well and which do not. Do more of what works and less of what doesn't.

You cannot manage what you cannot quantify. Most aspects of an internet company can be measured, so make use of this. It will inform you which advertisements are effective and which portions of your website want development. This knowledge is invaluable, so be sure you utilize it.

# CONCLUSION

We've listed the seven most typical errors that new internet company owners make that prohibit them from succeeding. Now that you're aware of these errors, you must resolve them to avoid doing them again. This is critical for the success of your internet company!

CONCLUSIÓN

www.ingramcontent.com/pod-product-compliance
Lightning Source LLC
Chambersburg PA
CBHW072058230526
45479CB00010B/1130